Jack the Ripper

Jack the Ripper

The code was on the Wall

ALLAN DOWNEY

Library of Congress Control Number: 2021900954

HARDBACK: 978-1-954673-23-6
PAPERBACK: 978-1-954673-22-9
EBOOK: 978-1-954673-24-3

Ordering Information:

For orders and inquiries, please contact:
1-888-404-1388
www.goldtouchpress.com
book.orders@goldtouchpress.com

Printed in the United States of America

Contents

Introduction

Walter Richard Sickert, the artist, was Jack the Ripper. Until now, nobody has been able to say what the chalk message written on the wall means. The chalk message written after a double murder said -

```
THE JUWES ARE
THE MEN THAT
WILL NOT
BE BLAMED
FOR NOTHING
```

This has been a mystery for 120 years.

This book reveals what the words represent when they are decoded. The following pages show the reason why these words were chosen and arranged the way they were and confirms that Walter Richard Sickert said that he was Jack the Ripper.

Motive for the Murders

Sir Charles Warren was appointed Chief Commissioner of the Metropolitan Police in 1886, two years before the murders started. Warren had been a decorated officer in the army before he was asked by Home Secretary, Hugh Childers, to accept the post of Chief Commissioner. The reason being that the previous commissioner resigned following severe censure by the Home Secretary because of trouble between the police and the unemployed. Warren was accused of militarizing the police and of being an inefficient martinet by the Pall Mall Gazette.

The following year, 1887, on the 20th November, known as Bloody Sunday, the police attacked marchers of unemployed heading for Trafalgar Square, leaving two dead and many injured. The following week another unemployed worker was killed by the police. The Grenadier Guards and the Life Guards were also involved at these demonstrations.

The leaders of the workers were, Annie Besant, MP Charles Bradlaugh and George Bernard Shaw. Walter Sickert knew these three people through his wife Ellen whose family the Cobden's were liberals. He painted Bradlaugh's portrait twice.

After Bloody Sunday, George Bernard Shaw wrote about the incident, the last sentence started, "It all comes from." Later Sickert did a painting entitled, 'It all comes from sticking to a soldier'. This shows that Sickert was reading about what was going on.

Sickert wanted to get rid of Sir Charles Warren by way of humiliating him and ruining his career. Warren resigned on the 8th November 1888. The next day, Lord Mayor's Day, Mary Kelly became Jack the Ripper's last victim.

The Message Written on the Wall

The layout of the words written on the wall was a clue that the twelve words contained another message. The usual way to write it would be 3 lines of 4 words or 4 lines of 3 words.

The first line contained 3 words as they stood for the 3 words in Jack the Ripper.

The second line contained 3 words as they stood for the 3 words in Walter Richard Sickert.

The other 6 words were laid out in 3 lines of 2 words so that the letters would be in the correct place.

The code is worked out by giving each letter in a word its equivalent number, for example, the word Juwes: J=1 U=2 W=3 E=4 S=5.

The numbers in the code connect with each other, e.g., 1234 or 3333, or 1212, or 1111.

The Writing on the Wall - What it Means

There are three words in the first line of the chalk message THE, JUWES and ARE. There are three words in Jack the Ripper. So the J in JUWES represents the J in Jack. THE is the, and the R in ARE represents the R in Ripper. First line = JACK THE RIPPER.

There are three more words in the second line, THE, MEN and THAT. The T in THE represents the T in Walter. The E in MEN represents the E in Sickert. The H and A in THAT represents the H and A in Richard. Second line = Walter Richard Sickert.

So now I will put Jack the Ripper in his place, which is at the end of the riddle, namely his signature. Walter Richard Sickert now becomes the first line.

The code is based on letters and numbers. The fifth letter in the word NOTHING is I. The fifth letter in the JUWES is S. Together they spell IS. The letters of the words are connected by the numbers, so from the letter I in the word nothing to the letter S in the word JUWES the connection is five to five. I then drew a line from the letter S up and above the word JUWES and then down and under the word THE. The letters in the word THE represent the numbers 1, 2, 3, i.e. T=1, H=2, E = 3. I then drew the line until I came to the letter N in the word MEN. N is the third letter in MEN, so the connection between E and N = three to three. I then drew the line down in front of the letter N until I came to the third letter in the word BLAMED. The connection between N to A = three to three. I then drew the line in front of and under the A until the letter E. Now the riddle reads - Walter Richard Sickert is the Name. I then drew the line between the O and R in the word FOR and then up and around the word THE on the second line, and then down and under the M in MEN and then up and around the U and then down and around the R in FOR, D and E in BLAMED and then up and around the R and E in ARE and then down and around the word BE and then up and around the Tin NOT and up and in between the letters A and T in THAT. I continued up and around the E and R in ARE and then up and around the E and down to the bottom, where I put Jack the Ripper and then between the C and Kin Jack and then up around the N and O in NOTHING and up and around the W in Will and then around the N in MEN and finally up and around the A in ARE and the S in JUWES. The riddle is decoded and reads

Walter Richard Sickert is the name of the murderer better known as Jack the Ripper.

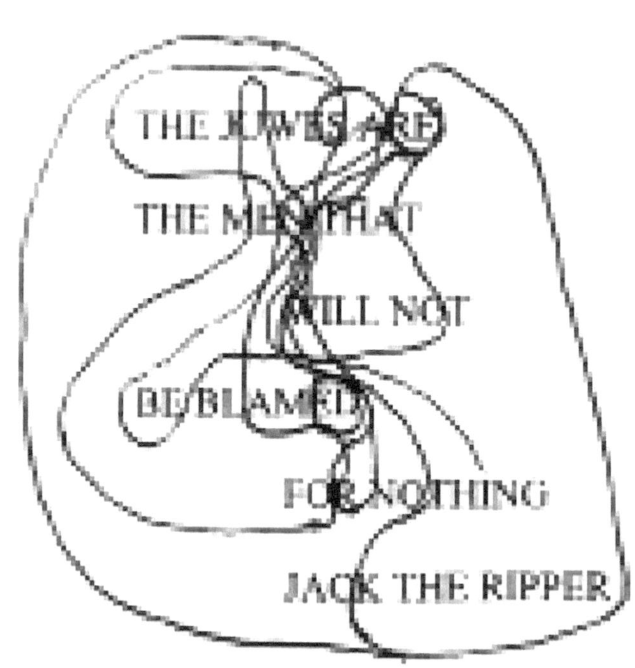

THE JUWES ARE
THE MEN THAT
WILL NOT
BE BLAMED
FOR NOTHING
JACK THE RIPPER

The Writing on the Wall

The position number of each letter in each word used is below.
The numbers for Walter= 333333.

```
WALTER  RICHARD  SICKERT
333333  1234126  5534321


IS  THE  NAME  OF  THE  MURDERER
55  123  3345  21  123  12365232


BETTER  KNOWN  AS  JACK  THE  RIPPER
123432  41213  15  1234  123  123456
```

Words used from the message written on the wall.

juWes blAmed wiLl noT arE fOR

RIpper jaCk notHing ARe blameD

juweS nothIng jaCK thE aRe The

nothIng juweS THE MeN blAMEd

nOt For THE

Men jUwes foR blameD blamEd aRe

arE aRe

BE noT thaT arE aRe

jacK NOthing WIll meN Are juweS

JACK THE RIPPER

Some months later, as I was reading through 'Portrait of a Killer' again, I looked at a map in the book, which showed the locality of the murders. This map was printed in the Daily Telegraph on Saturday November 10th, 1888, which was the day after Mary Kelly was murdered. I thought that the murderer was operating from a base somewhere between the murder sites. I noticed that Old Montague Street was in the centre of the map and about an equal distance from all the murder sites. I then saw that the chalk message and some of the Ripper letters contained the letters to spell base at Old Montague Street.

So the chalk message written on the wall contained this message, Walter Richard Sickert, base at Old Montague Street, is the name of the murderer, better known as Jack the Ripper

The position number of each letter in each word used is below.

BASE AT OLD MONTAGUE STREET
1253 34 236 12341723 543321

Words used,

Be jAck juweS thE thAT

nOt wiLl blameD

Men nOt meN thaT Are nothinG jUwes thE

juweS thaT foR thE mEn That

In the words, base Old Montague, the numbers 5, 6, 7 are out of place in their respective word, but they connect with each other.

Sickert was a friend of Oscar Wilde for some years and both of them despised the ruling class. Wilde's novel, "THE PICTURE OF DORIAN GRAY", was published in 1890, which was over one year since Mary Kelly, the last victim, was murdered on the 9th November 1888. I looked at Wilde's novel to see if there was anything in the text that might indicate something about Sickert. I found on the first page the same message that I found in Jack the Ripper's writings, i.e., Walter Richard Sickert, based at Old Montague Street, is the name of the murderer, better known as Jack the Ripper. The first sentence of the book is an anagram of Walter Richard Sickert.

The position number of each letter in each word used is below.

WALTER RICHARD SICKERT
123123 1234234 1234567

```
BASE AT OLD MONTAGUE STREET
1234 12  123  12345678  123456
```

```
IS THE NAME OF THE MURDERER
23 123  1234 12  123  12345678
```

```
BETTER KNOWN AS JACK THE RIPPER
123456 12345  12  1234  123  123456
```

Words on first page of 'The Picture of Dorian Gray', Chapter 1, in order,

WAs liLac The hEavy moRe

RICH gARDen

Studio rICh pinK   fillEd floweRing

delicaTe

Blossoms gArden roSEs AT   Odour

fLowering saDdle

MOmentary   wiNd   wotTon   fantAstic

stragGling dreadfUl

anywherE

STirred moRe treEs therE amidsT

hIS THE Now fAntastic moMEntary

OF THE

More sUmmer gaRDEn floweRing perfumE

momentaRy

Blossoms dElicate woTTon summER

Kind aNd flOWering thorN AS

JApanese riCh pinK

THE RIch opPressive peoPle flowERing

The "rich oppressive people flowering" seems to indicate a political motive for the murders. In the excerpt of Chapter 1 of 'The Picture of Dorian Gray' the above referenced words are underlined. On the third page, the first sentence is, "Dorian Gray? Is that his name?" asked Lord Henry, walking across the studio towards **Basil Hallward.**

BaSIl HAllWARD stands for Walter Richard Sickert.

WA, for Walter, HARD, for Richard, SI, for Sickert.

The sentence decoded says, Oscar Wilde Walter Richard Sickert

OSCAR WILDE WALTER RICHARD SICKERT
23232 12343 123123 2222334 2223432

Words used in sentence in order,

tOwards baSil a Cross grAy gRay

Walking hIs haLlward stuDio thE

WALking That hEnry doRian

gRay hIs aCross tHAt loRD

iS hIs aCross asKed namE loRd sTudio

Dorian Gray seems to stand for Oscar Wilde.

The following are excerpts from 'The Picture of Dorian Gray' by Oscar Wilde. The first is from Chapter 1 and the second excerpt is from the last chapter of the book. Words highlighted in **bold** are those that are used in the above code.

The **studio** was <u>filled</u> with **the** <u>rich</u> <u>odour</u> of <u>roses,</u> <u>and</u> when the <u>light</u> <u>summer</u> <u>wind</u> <u>stirred</u> <u>amidst</u> the <u>trees</u> <u>of</u> **the** <u>garden,</u> <u>there</u> came through the open door the <u>heavy</u> scent of the <u>lilac,</u> or **the** <u>more delicate</u> <u>perfume</u> of the <u>pink-flowering</u> <u>thorn.</u>

From the corner of the divan of Persian <u>saddle</u>-bags on which he was lying, smoking, <u>as</u> was **his** custom, innumerable cigarettes, **Lord Henry** <u>Wotton</u> could just catch the gleam of the honey-sweet and honey- coloured <u>blossoms</u> of a laburnum, whose tremulous branches seemed hardly able to bear the burden of a beauty so flame-like as theirs ; and <u>now</u> and then the <u>fantastic</u> shadows of birds in flight flitted across the long tussore-silk curtains **that** were stretched in front of the huge window, producing a <u>kind</u> of <u>momentary Japanese</u> effect, and making him think of those pallid jade-faced painters of Tokio who, through the medium of an art that is necessarily immobile, seek to convey the sense of swiftness and motion. The sullen murmur of the bees shouldering their way through the long unmown grass, or circling with monotonous insistence round the dusty gilt horns of the <u>straggling</u> woodbine, seemed to make the stillness more <u>oppressive</u>. The dim roar of London was like the bourdon note of a distant organ.

In the centre of the room, clamped to an upright easel, stood the full- length portrait of a young man of extraordinary personal beauty, and in front of it, some little distance away, was sitting the artist himself, Basil **Hallward,** whose sudden disappearance some years ago caused, <u>at</u> the time, such public excitement, and gave rise to so many strange conjectures.

As the painter looked at the gracious and comely form he had so skillfully mirrored in his art, a smile of pleasure passed across his face, and seemed about to linger there. But he suddenly started up, and, closing his eyes, placed his fingers upon the lids, as though he sought to imprison within his brain some curious dream from which he feared he might awake.

"It is your best work, Basil, the best thing you have ever done," said **Lord Henry,** languidly. "You must certainly send it next year to the Grosvenor. The Academy is too large and too vulgar. Whenever I have gone there, there have been either so many <u>people</u> that I have not been able to see the pictures, which was <u>dreadful,</u> or so many pictures that I have not been able to see the people, which was worse. The Grosvenor is really the only place."

"I don't think I shall send it anywhere," he answered, tossing his head back in that odd way that used to make his friends laugh at him at Oxford. "No: I won't send it <u>anywhere.</u>"

Lord Henry elevated his eyebrows, and looked at him in amazement through the thin blue wreaths of smoke that curled *The Picture of Dorian Gray, Chapter 1*

> ... He had cleaned it many times, **till** there **was no** stain left upon it. It **was** bright, and glistened. **As** it had killed **the** painter, **so** it would **kill** the painter's work, and all **that** that meant. It would kill the past and when that was dead he would **be** free. It would kill this **monstrous** soul-life, and, **without** its **hideous** warnings, he would be at peace. He seized the thing, and stabbed the **picture** with it.

There was a cry heard, and a crash. The cry was so horrible in its **agony** that the frightened **servants** woke, and crept out of their rooms. Two gentlemen, who were passing in the **Square** below, **stopped**, and looked up at the great house. They walked on till they met a **policeman**, and brought him back. The man rang the bell several times, **but** there was no **answer. Except** for a light in one of the **top** windows, the house was all **dark.** After a **time,** he went away and stood in an **adjoining** portico and watched.

"Whose house is that, constable?" asked the elder of the two gentlemen. "Mr. Dorian Gray's, sir," **answered** the policeman.

They looked at each other, as they walked away, and **sneered.** One of them was Sir Henry Ashton's uncle.

Inside, in the servants' part of the house, the half-clad domestics were talking in low whispers to each other. Old Mrs. Leaf was **crying** and wringing her hands. Francis was as pale as death.

After about **quarter** of an hour, he got the coachman and one of the footmen and crept upstairs. They knocked, but there was no **reply.** They called out. **Everything** was **still.** Finally, after vainly trying to **force** the door, they got on the roof, and dropped down onto the balcony. The windows **yielded** easily; their bolts were **old.**

When they entered they found, hanging upon the wall, a splendid **portrait** of their master as they had last seen him, in all the **wonder** of his exquisite youth and beauty. Lying on the floor was a dead man, in evening dress, with a knife in his heart. He was withered, wrinkled, and loathsome of visage. It was not till they had examined the rings that they recognized who it was.

The Picture of Dorian Gray, Last Page

Then at the bottom of the third page,

"Well, I **will tell** you what it is. I want you to explain to me why you won't **exhibit Dorian Gray's picture. I want** the **real** reason."

The sentences decoded say,

Oscar Wilde Walter Richard

The position number of each letter in each word used is below.

OSCAR WILDE WALTER RICHARD
22333 12312 123123 1233321

Words used are from the sentence referred to above.. These words are in bold.

dOrian iS piCture grAy' s doRian

WILl Dorian tEll wAnt wiLl TEll doRian

Real pIcture exHibit reAl gRay's Dorian

On the last page, there is the same message as on the first page. The position number of each letter in each word used is below.

WALTER RICHARD SICKERT
123456 1234567 1234567

BASE AT OLD MONTAGUE STREET
1234 12 123 12345666 123456

IS THE NAME OF THE MURDERER
12 123 1234 12 123 12345666

BETTER KNOWN AS JACK THE RIPPER
123456 12345 12 3454 123 123456

Words used are from the previous excerpt of the last chapter of 'The Picture of Dorian Gray' and are in **bold..**

WAs tiLl lasT wondER

Reply yIelded piCture witHered servAnts

masteR sneereD

So kIll piCture darK answER withouT

But wAS excEpt AT OLD

MONstrous porTrait servAnts cryinG

hideOUs policEman

STill foRce werE mastEr everyThing

IS THE No dArk tiME OF THE

Master qUarter foRce wonDER policEman

answeRed

BE wiThout thaT answER

Kill aNd agOny ansWered cryiNg AS

adJoining squAre poliCeman darK

THE Reply tills toP stoPped answER

Wilde gave many clues in his novel that Sickert was Jack the Ripper. Dorian Gray murders Basil Hallward on the 9th of November and Mary Kelly was murdered on the 9th of November. Hallward had a Gladstone bag with him when he was murdered and Sickert owned a Gladstone bag. The East End and Whitechapel areas are mentioned. Lady Alice Chapman is a character in the book and Annie Chapman was a victim of Jack the Ripper. Alice and Annie have the same number of letters.

A character named Harden lives in Richmond. Richmond and Harden is an anagram of Richard. Taken from the book, "Dorian," he said "my letter don't be frightened-was to tell you that Sibyl Vane is dead." Don't be frightened is the postscript in the Ripper letter to the police on November 15th 1888. In 'The Secret Life of Oscar Wilde', a biography by Neil McKenna, Ada Leverson, a successful novelist and friend of Wilde, visited Wilde at the Albemarle Hotel in London where Wilde was staying in 1895. She recalled years later, "I saw a knife lying on a table in Oscar's rooms" "I **asked** him who left it there." "Oh, some careless young murderer," he said.

Sickert, like Oscar Wilde, and George Bernard Shaw, was a friend of Sergei Mikhailovich Kravchinski, who was better known as Stepnyak, a Russian revolutionary of noble birth who assassinated General Mezentsev, chief of the Russian secret police. Sickert's father is known to have hated authority, especially the police, and the letters of Jack the Ripper show clearly that Sickert hated the police also. Wilde and Shaw were socialists and knew one another for several years before the murders began. Sickert was a friend of Wilde and Wilde had been a friend of Sickert's father.

Sickert's father had been active politically before he moved to England in 1868, from Munich, where Sickert was born in 1860.

An anonymous letter of October 20, 1888, has definitely been written by Sickert. It read, " The motive for the crimes is hatred and spite against the authorities of Scotland Yard, one of whom is marked as a victim."

This letter decoded says,

Walter Richard Sickert, Old Montague Street

The position number of each letter in each word used is below.

WALTER RICHARD SICKERT OLD MONTAGUE STREET
125454 2331234 1234543 554 12231223 676554

Words used,

Whom mArked scotLand spiTE hatRed

cRImes viCtim HAtred foR yarD

Spite vICtim marKEd hatRed moTive

authOrities scotLand yarD

MOtive aNd haTred AGainst aUthorities thE

againST authoRities hatrEd spitE vicTim

Sickert was telling the police his name in the letters. This was his way of saying that the police were fools because they could not see it.

"Ha Ha Ha" "Catch me if you can" "It's a jolly nice lark" "What a dance I am leading" The last two sentences = Walter Richard Sickert

One letter sent to the police is signed-

"Jack a Poland Jew better known as Jack the Ripper"

When Jack the Ripper wrote, "Would you like to catch me? I guess you would well look here", he meant look in the letter.

I first became interested in the mystery surrounding the identity of Jack the Ripper when I read 'Portrait of a Killer - Jack the Ripper - Case Closed' by Patricia Cornwell. After reading this book I looked back to the part where Jack the Ripper left a chalk message written on a wall soon after committing two murders within one hour. I then attempted to see if I could discover a meaning behind these words.

The words written on the wall - The Juwes are The men That Will not be Blamed for nothing - seemed to me to contain a hidden meaning. It only took me ten minutes to decode this riddle.

The first thing that struck me was the word Juwes. I thought that it was spelled this way so that the letter u would be included and the word murder then used in the decoded message.

Jack the Ripper wrote many letters to the police and used the expression Ha Ha in many of them. In her book, Patricia Cornwell says that the Ha Ha's found in the Ripper letters could have been taken from the artist James McNeill Whistler's frequent use of them. Sickert had been an apprentice to Whistler in 1884, four years before the murders began. In fact the Ha Ha's were taken from Dostoevsky's novel Crime and Punishment as were the words in the chalk message written on the wall.

The NAME Jack the Ripper was taken from

the Dostoevsky novel The Idiot,

Penguin Classics page 208,

Japanese bACK the RIP hapPens cleveRly.

On the 30th September, the fifth victim, Catherine Eddowes was found murdered in Mitre Square, Aldgate, at 1.44 a.m. by P.C. Edward Watkins. At 2.55 a.m. a piece of her apron, still wet with blood, was found lying in the entry to Nos. 108-119 Wentworth Model Dwellings by PC Alfred Long, a Metropolitan Police constable on duty in Goulston Street, Whitechapel. Just inside the doorway, on the right-hand side, the chalk message was written with white chalk on the black dado of the wall, just above the apron. The murderer left the apron there as his calling card to show that he had written the chalk message on the wall.

The first Ripper victim was Martha Tabram who was 39 years old and was stabbed to death 39 times, 38 of them with a penknife and 1 with a large knife or dagger or bayonet. This indicates that 39 was the chosen number of stab wounds and not a random number. This was a first clue as numbers were used in connection with the other murders and in the Ripper's letters and the chalk message written on the wall.

Jack the Ripper murdered six women, all of them prostitutes, in a three month period in 1888, all of them within a fifteen minute walk of Old Montague Street in the east end of London. Martha Tabram was the first victim to be murdered on the 7th August at George Yard Buildings, a tenement block in George Yard (present Gunthorpe Street), off Whitechapel High Street. Heading north west from George Yard, Old Montague is a five minute walk.

This first murder was nearer to Old Montague Street than any of the five murders that followed it. The second victim was Mary Ann Nichols, murdered at Buck's Row (now Durward Street), Whitechapel. Heading south west from Buck's Row, Old Montague Street is less than a ten-minute walk. The third victim was Annie Chapman, murdered on 8th September in the backyard of 29 Hanbury Street, Spitalfields. Heading south east from Hanbury Street, Old Montague Street is. a ten-minute walk. The fourth victim was Elizabeth Stride, murdered on 30th September in the passage leading from Bemer Street to a small court known as Dutfield's Yard. Berner Street is in Whitechapel. Heading north from Bemer Street Old Montague Street is a ten-minute walk. The fifth victim was Catherine Eddowes, murdered in Mitre Square in the City of London.

Heading north east from Mitre Square, Old Montague Street is between a ten and fifteen minute walk. After this murder Jack the Ripper walked to Goulston Street, which is on the way to Old Montague Street. Here at Nos. 108 to 119 Wentworth Dwellings, Goulston Street, Jack the Ripper left on the ground a bloody piece of apron he took from Catherine Eddowes and above it on the right hand wall, which was just inside the doorway, he wrote in white chalk on the black dado of the wall, The Juwes are The men That Will not be Blamed for nothing

From Goulston Street to the start of Old Montague Street it is just a five - minute walk. The sixth victim was Mary Jane Kelly, murdered in Miller's Court off Dorset Street, Spitalfields. Heading south east from Miller's Court, Old Montague Street is a ten-minute walk.

The dates of the murders are significant. The three murders that occurred on the dates, the 7th August, the 8th September and the 9th November are connected. August is the 8th month, September the 9th month. So the numbers connected to the murders are 7th of the 8th, 8th of the 9th, 9th of the eleventh. The murders occurred in that order, the 7th being the first murder, the 8th the second and the 9th the third. So the 7th= 1, 8th= 2, 9th= 3.

Of the three other murders that occurred, two of them, on the 30th September and one on the 31st August, are connected by 30 and 31. As the two murders that happened on the 30th took place after murders on the 31st, they were the second murders in this sequence. So the 30th= 2 and the 31st = 1. The sequence of numbers for the murders is; 1, 2, 3, 2, 1. The dates are 7, 8, 9, 30, 31.

Stephen Knight in his book, 'Jack the Ripper The Final Solution', states that Sickert knew Mary Kelly. Knight says that Sickert rented rooms in a great red-brick terrace house at 15 Cleveland Street and was the catalyst in getting Mary Kelly a job in a confectioner and tobacconist's shop at 22 Cleveland Street. Later Sickert asked Mary Kelly to take a job as a nanny in the basement of 6 Cleveland Street. A letter sent by Jack the Ripper and received by the police on the 8th October 1889, was written with the postscript at the top of the page. This was done for a reason, for the words in the postscript form the anagram, From Cleveland Street.

P.S I hope you can read what I <u>have</u> **written, and** will <u>put</u> it <u>all</u> in <u>the</u> paper, not <u>leave</u> <u>half out</u>. If you can not <u>see</u> **the** letters let <u>me know</u> and I will <u>write</u> <u>them</u> bigger.

Dear **Sir**

I shall be in **Whitechapel** on the 20th of this month- and will begin some very **delicate** work about midnight, in the street where I executed my third examination of the human body.

Yours **till death Jack** the **Ripper Catch** Me if you can

This letter decoded has the following message:

Walter Richard Sickert based at 20 Old Montague Street is the name of the murderer better known as Jack the Ripper

The words used are underlined in the 8th October 1889 letter excerpted above. The postscript decoded:

halF wRite knOw Me

Can aLl thE leaVe havE Leave cAN reaD

P.S. puT wRite thEm sEe noT

The position number of each letter in each word used is below.

```
FROM CLEVELAND STREET
4231 123441234 232323
```

Letter decoded from the previously excerpted 8th October 1889 letter with the words used marked in bold.

Whitechapel jAck tiLl deaTh RippER
Ripper Catch tHe And wRitten Death

SIr JaCK RippEr rippeR delicaTe

The position number of each letter in each word used is below.

```
WALTER RICHARD SICKERT
123456 1212121 1234567
```

Words used are taken from the 8th October 1889 excerpted previously.

Begin About Shall Executed Delicate

And This abOut deLicate miDnight

MONTh humAn beGin hUman Executed

The position number of each letter in each word used is below.

```
BASED AT OLD MONTAGUE STREET
11111 11 333 12344321 123456
```

```
IS THE NAME OF THE MURDERER
34 123 1234 12 123 12345612
```

```
BETTER KNOWN AS JACK THE RIPPER
123456 12345 67 1234 123 123456
```

Words used are taken from the 8th October 1889 excerpted above.

thIS Not cAn huMan papEr

MOnth hUman veRy reaD RippER Executed

wRitten

BE noT wriTten streEt letteRs

KNOW humaN delicAte letterS

Soon after the Hanbury Street murder, other messages began to be chalked up on the walls in the vicinity of the crime. On a wall in a passage running off Hanbury Street, one message foretold that it would get worse.

```
    THIS IS THE FOURTH. I WILL MURDER
    16 MORE AND THEN GIVE MYSELF UP.
```

The murders in this message add up to 20, and the Ripper letter received by police on 8th October 1889, suggests that his base was at 20 Old Montague Street.

This message decoded says,

Walter Old Montague Street

The position number of each letter in each word used is below.

```
WALTER OLD MONTAGUE STREET
113133 234 12211123 456545
```

Ripper Letter
HA!Ha!Ha!. "To tell you the truth you ought to be obliged to me for killing such a deuced lot of vermin, why they are ten times worse than men

This letter decoded says

```
Walter Richard Sickert based at
Old Montague Street is the name
of the murderer Catch me when
you can
```

The position number of each letter in each word used is below.

```
WALTER RICHARD SICKERT
123432 3434321 1231234

BASED AT OLD MONTAGUE STREET
23456 11 111 12343333 443321

IS THE NAME OF THE MURDERER
45 123 3333 12 123 12312323

CATCH ME WHEN YOU CAN
43434 12 1234 123 434
```

<u>Words used</u>:

Why ʜA teLl truTh thE aRe

woRse obLIged suCH thAn tRuth Deuced

Such tImes suCh Killing mEn veRmin truTh

oBliged thAn worSE deuceD Are To

Of Lot Deuced

Me tO teN truTh thAn ouGht yoU thE

worSe truTh foR thEy tEll Ten

oblIged timeS meN thAn tiMes arE

Me sUch foR DEuced veRmin tEn foR

deuCed thAn truTh suCH

WHy thEy thaN deuCed thAN

The word deuce is used more than once in 'Crime and Punishment'.

A letter, with part of a kidney enclosed, was sent to Mr George Lusk, chairman of the Whitechapel Vigilance Committee, which had been set up to patrol the streets after the murder of Annie

Chapman. It reads,

> From hell Mr Lusk **Sir**
>
> I **send** you **half** the **Kidne** I took from one **woman praserved it** for **you tother piece I fried and ate** it **was very nise.** I **may send** you the **bloody** knif **that** took it **out** if you **only** wate a whil **longer signed**
>
> **Catch** me when you can
>
> **Mishter** Lusk

This letter decoded says

> Walter Richard Sickert, base at Old Montague Street, is the name of the murderer, Catch me if you can

The position number of each letter in each word used is below.

```
WALTER RICHARD SICKERT BASE AT OLD MONTAGUE
STREET  123456  2345123  1111234  1234  12  123
12343333  123451
```

Words used are taken from the 'From Hell' letter and have been marked in **bold.**

WAs haLf thaT piecE totheR

fRied catCH Ate pRasarved anD

Sir It Catch Kidne sEnd veRy thaT

Bloody mAy niSE ATe

Only bLoody kiDne

May wOman seNd thaT thAt siGned yoU thE

Sir iT veRy nisE tothEr Took

nISe THE

Nise hAlf woMan nisE One iF THE

May oUt veRy senD piecE longeR mishtER

SIgnED CAtCH me When you cAn MishTER LusK contains the words Walter Richard Sickert.

The position number of each letter in each word used in the "From Hell" letter is below.

```
IS THE NAME OF THE MURDERER
23 123 1234 12 123 12345667
```

"Just to give you a little clue" "I told her I was Jack the Ripper and I took my hat off" "Hold on tight you cunning lot of coppers" "Goodbye for the present from the Ripper and the Dodger" Decoded it reads:

```
walter Richard Sickert, base at
Old Montague Street, is the name
of the murderer, better known as
Jack the Ripper
```

Letter decoded

WAs toLd litTle RippER

RIpper JaCk HAt heR GooD

JuSt lIttle Clue JacK thE heR liTtle

Bye wAS cluE hAT tOLD

My tO cuNning litTle And cunninG

JUst thE

copperS presenT coppeRs litTlE coppErs

tighT

gIve waS cuNning wAs My hEr Off

My jUst heR tolD RippER littlE

RippeR

Bye hEr liTTle RippER

JacK cuNning tO Was aNd wAS

JACK THE RIPPER

The position number of each letter in each word used is below.

WALTER RICHARD SICKERT
123456 1231234 3214333

BASE AT OLD MONTAGUE STREET
1234 23 234 12341723 776655

IS THE NAME OF THE MURDERER
23 123 3212 12 123 12345666

BETTER KNOWN AS
123456 43212 23

JACK THE RIPPER
1234 123 123456

Letter of 25th September - The First Letter to be Signed "Jack the Ripper"

Dear Boss

I keep on hearing the police have caught me but they wont fix me just yet. I have laughed when they look so clever and talk about being on the right track. That joke about a leather apron gave me real fits. I am down on whores and I shant quit ripping them till I do get buckled. Grand work, the last job was, I gave the lady no time to squeal. How can they catch me now. I love my work and want to start again. You will soon hear of me with my funny little games. I saved some of the proper red stuff in a ginger beer bottle over the last job to write with but it went thick like glue and

I couldn't use it. Red ink is fit enough I hope ha ha. The next job I do I shall clip the lady's ears off and send to the police officers just for jolly wouldn't you. Keep this letter back till I do a bit more work then give it out straight. My knife's so nice and sharp and I want to get to work right away if I get a chance. Good luck.

Yours truly Jack the Ripper. Don't mind me giving the trade name. Wasn't good enough to post this before I got all the red ink off my hands curse it. No luck yet. They say I'm a doctor now ha ha.

The first sentence with Dear Boss contains the letters to spell WALTER RICHARD SICKERT. The second, fourth, tenth and thirteenth sentences also contain the letters to spell his full name. The fifth, eighth and ninth sentences contain the letters to spell WALTER. Combining the eleventh and twelfth sentences produces WALTER RICHARD SICKERT, as do the fourteenth and fifteenth. Yours truly Jack the Ripper = SICKERT, and the last three sentences - WALTER RICHARD SICKERT.

"Ripper" Letter to the Police

Reasons for Supposing Jack

the ripper a tailor from his letter, first (Ripper) is a tailors word (Buckle) a tailors word they won't (fix) fix buttons (proper red stuff) army cloth or suits (real fits) tailors words-good fits men generally use expressions borrowed from their trade

Yours truly Mathematicus

This letter decoded says,

> Walter Richard Sickert, base at Old Montague Street, is the name of the murderer, better known as Jack the Ripper

The position number of each letter in each word used is below.

```
WALTER RICHARD SICKERT
121121 1231234 1234561


BASE AT OLD MONTAGUE STREET
1234 23 543 12341111 654321


IS THE NAME OF THE MURDERER
12 123 3212 21 123 12345654


BETTER KNOWN AS JACK THE RIPPER
1234456 43213 34 1234 123 123456
```

Words used in letter, in order.

Word jAck Letter Tailor rEasons Reasons

Reasons rIpper jaCk His tAilors fiRst

worD

Supposing rIpper jaCK rippER The

Buckle tAilors hiS gonE mAThematicus

tailOr taiLor reD

Men wONT Army Generally Use Expressions

suppoSing firsT expRessions thE rEasons

Tailors

IS THE

woNt tAilors MEn fOr For THE

Men sUpposing woRD rippER lettEr

expRessions

Buckle 1ETTER

jaCK woNt wOnt Wont meN reASons

JACK THE RIPPER

This letter indicates that Sickert took words from 'Crime and Punishment', as the word Supposing is spelled with a capital S instead of a small s as it should have been. In 'Crime and Punishment'; the word Supposing is spelled 3 times with a capital S.

Ripper Letter to the Police
15th November 1888

excuse paper
cannot afford to
Buy any

Dear Boss

I **Shall Be at my work** in **City Road** on **Monday**
Jack the Ripper

Don't be **Frightened**

This letter decoded says,

> Walter Richard Sickert, base at Old
> Montague Street, is the name of
> the murderer, better known as Jack
> the Ripper Catch me if you can

The position number of each letter in each word used is below.

```
WALTER RICHARD SICKERT
124456 1232344 1234566


BASE AT OLD MONTAGUE STREET
1212 12 456 12333444 123456


IS THE NAME OF THE MURDERER
11 123 3212 12 123 12345665


BETTER KNOWN AS JACK THE RIPPER
123456 43212 34 1234 123 123456


CATCH ME IF YOU CAN
12312 12 12 444 123
```

Words used in the 15th November letter are marked above in bold.

Work pAper shaLl donT rippER

RIpper jaCk sHAll deaR roaD

Shall cIty jaCK rippER cannoT

Buy pAper Shall bE AT

affOrd shalL afforD

MONday ciTy shAll friGhtened excUse papEr

Shall aT woRk papEr rippEr frighTened

I Shall THE

caNnot pAper My dEar On aFford THE

Monday bUy woRk roaD rippER excusE

papeR

BE ciTy donT rippER

jacK caNnot tO Work oN deAr bosS

Jack the Ripper

cAnnot ciTy City sHall Monday bE

I aFford citY affOrd excUse CANnot

"Ripper" Letter to the Police
Posted on 22nd July 1889

London West Dear Boss

Back again & up to the old tricks. Would
you like to catch me? I guess you would
well look here - I leave my diggings close
to Conduit St to night at about 10:30 watch
Conduit St & close round there-Ha-Har I dare
you 4 more lives four more cunts to add to
my little collection & I shall rest content
Do what you will you will never nap. Not a
big blade but sharp

Jack the Ripper

This letter decoded says,

Walter Richard Sickert, base at
Old Montague Street, is the name

> of the murderer, better known
> as Jack the Ripper Catch me if
> you can

The position number of each letter in each word used is below.

```
WALTER RICHARD SICKERT
123456 1231234 1234567
```

```
BASE AT OLD MONTAGUE STREET
1234 12 123 12341234 123455
```

```
IS THE NAME OF THE MURDERER
56 123 1212 11 123 12345654
```

```
BETTER KNOWN AS JACK THE RIPPER
123456 43211 11 1234 123 123456
```

```
CATCH ME IF YOU CAN
12345 12 11 123 123
```

Words used in the 22nd July 1889 letter are marked in bold above.

WAtch weLl cunTs rippER

RIpper jaCk HAR blaDe

Sharp rIpper jaCK rippER collecTion

BAck reSt herE

AT OLD

MOre coNTent AGain roUnd herE

ST heRE rippEr abouT

diggIngs trickS THE NAME

Old Four THE

More cUnts heRe blaDe rippER bladE shaRp

Back mE liTTle rippER

jacK coNtent tO Watch Night Again Shall

JACK THE RIPPER

CATCH ME

I Four YOU CAtch cuNts

In the first sentence, "the tricks" is an anagram of Sickert.

Postcard to Central News
Received 1st October 1888

I **was not** codding dear **old** Boss **when** I **gave** you **the** tip, you'll hear **about saucy** Jacky s **work tomorrow** double **event this time** number **one** squealed a **bit couldn't finish straight off. had** not time to get **ears** for **police** thanks for **keeping last letter** back till I got to **work again,**

Jack the Ripper

This postcard decoded says,

> Walter Richard Sickert, base at Old Montague Street, is the name of the murderer, better known as Jack the Ripper

```
WALTER RICHARD SICKERT
123456 1231234 1234567

BASE AT OLD MONTAGUE STREET
1234 12 123 34341234 123123

IS THE NAME OF THE MURDERER
45 123 1234 12 123 33333333

BETTER KNOWN AS JACK THE RIPPER
123456 43212 23 1234 123 123456
```

Words used in the 1st October postcard are marked in bold above.

WAs poLice lasT lettER

RIpper jaCk HAd woRk codDing

Saucy rIpper jaCK rippER couldn'T

Bit wAS gavE About sTraight OLD

toMOrrow fiNish lasT AGain saUcy timE

sTRaight Event kEeping leTter

FinISh THis onE

Not gAve toMorrow timE OFf THE

toMorrow saUcy woRk haD whEn eaRs evEnt

woRk

Bit 1ETTER

jacK fINish wOrk Was oNe 1ASt

JACK THE RIPPER

"Ripper" Letter to Dr. Thomas Openshaw Curator of the Pathology Museum of the London Hospital

This letter was posted in London on 29th October 1888 and addressed to Dr Openshaw at the London Hospital in Whitechapel.

Old boss you was rite it was **the left kidny I was goin to hopperate agin close to your ospitle** just as I was goin to dror **mi nife** along of er **bloomin throte** them **cusses** of **coppers spoilt** the **game** but I **guess** i **wil** be on the job soon and will send you another bit of innerds

Jack the **ripper**

O **have** you seen the devle with his mikerscope and scalpul a lookin at a Kidney with a slide cocked up

This letter decoded says,

> walter Richard Sickert, base at Old Montague Street, is the name of the murderer, better known as Jack the Ripper

```
WALTER RICHARD SICKERT
123456 1231234 1234566

BASE AT OLD MONTAGUE STREET
1234 12 123 12341123 123456

IS THE NAME OF THE MURDERER
12 123 1234 23 123 12345677

BETTER KNOWN AS JACK THE RIPPER
123456 12312 12 1234 123 123456
```

Words used in the 29th October 1888 letter are marked in bold in letter ..

WAs wiL anoTher rippER

RIpper jaCk HAve thRote senD

Send rIpper jaCK rippER spoilT

Boss wAS ritE Agin iT

OLD

Mi cOppers seNd anoTher And GUEss

Spoilt iT thRote ritE closE spoilT

It oSpitle THE

Nife gAME yOu leFt THEm

Mi cUsses thRote senD hoppERate ospitlE

anotheR

Bloomin sEnd biT anoTher coppERs

Kidny aNother Will aNd Agin oSpitle

JACK THE RIPPER

Ripper Letter to the Press
11th September 1889

"Dear Sir **Please will** you **oblige me** by **putting this into your paper** to **let the** people **of** England **now** (know) that I **hum** (am) **still living** and **running at larg as yet."**

Jack the Ripper

The words in bold above are those used in the code. This letter decoded says,

```
Walter Richard Sickert, base at
Old Montague Street, is the name
of the murderer, better known as
Jack the Ripper
```

The position number of each letter in each word used is below.

```
WALTER RICHARD SICKERT
123345  1231231  1234561

BASE AT OLD MONTAGUE STREET
2345 12 111 11224433 121234

IS THE NAME OF THE MURDERER
34 123 1234 12 123 12312345

BETTER KNOWN AS JACK THE RIPPER
123445 12345 12 1234 123 123456
```

Words used in the 11th September 1889 letter are marked in **bold.**

Will pAper obLige inTo papER

RIpper jaCk Hum 1ARg Dear

Still 1Iving jaCK rippER The

oBlige deAr thiS rippEr AT

Oblige Let Dear

Me Oblige iNto sTill pleAse larG yoUr

plEase

STill Running yEt plEase putTing

thIS THE

Now pAper huM papEr OF THE

Me pUtting laRg DEar siR papER

By dEar puTTing papER

KNOW liviNg AS

JACK THE RIPPER

On Page 13th, the decode is incomplete for the anonymous letter dated October 20th, 1888. This letter decoded says,

Walter Richard Sickert, Old Montague Street, is the name of the murderer and the name of the one marked as a victim is Mary Kelly.

Words used,

Is the aNd agAinst criMEs of the Motive

aUthorities

yaRD

hatrEd authoRities spitE hatRed and the

aNd agAinst criMEs of the one marked as a victim is

MARked Yard marKEd scotLand scotLand

Yard

Anonymous Letter
to the City of London Police
Dated 20th November 1888

"Look at the case in **County Durham** ... **twas made** to **appear** as **if** it was **Jack the Ripper"**

The words in bold above are those used in the code. This letter decoded says,

> Mary Kelly is dead and now my
> work is finished Walter Richard
> Sickert, Catch me if you can

The position number of each letter in each word used is below.

```
WALTER RICHARD SICKERT MARY KELLY IS DEAD
121233 1234561 3234565 6566 45116 23 34 33
```

```
CATCH ME IF YOU CAN AND NOW MY WORK IS
FINISHED
12112 14 12 623 124 543 432 66 1234 23 21223443
```

Words used in the 20th November are marked in **bold.,**

WAs Look aT thE duRham

RIpPer jaCk durHAm appeaR Durham

waS rIpPer jaCK rippER counTy

CAse Twas County tHe Made appEar

IF countY cOUnty cAse couNty

DurhaM appeAR countY jacK rippEr

Look Look countY

RIpper caSe maDE twAs rnaDe

AppeAr couNty maDe couNty loOk tWas

DurhaM countY Was cOuntry duRham jacK

RIpper caSe iF IN r8pper caSe durHam

appEar maDe

Ripper Letter
of 29th September 1888
From Liverpool

"Beware, I **shall** be at work on the 1st and 2nd inst, in **Minories** at **twelve midnight**, and I give the authorities a good chance, but **there is never** a **policeman near** when I am at work."

The words in bold above are those used in the code that spells CLEVELAND STREET. This is referred to in the second letter that was received after the double murder of 30th September 1888.

In the first sentence of "The Picture of Dorian Gray" on Page 9, the decode should contain, Mary Kelly is dead and now my work is finished. Also, it should be in the Ripper letters on pages 16,19,25,27. The decode on Page 8 should contain the artist Whitechapel.

Page 9, aMidst heAvy stiRred heavY pinK scEnt fiLLed heavY rIch roSes Door hEAvy stuDio AND piNk flOWering summMer heavY Wind mORe pinK rIch roSes FIlled piNk delIcate roses ricH fillED. On page 30 the ripper letter decode should contain, and the name of the one marked as a victim is

Mary Kelly. Decode for chalk message, Walter Richard Sickert the artist base at Old Montague

Street Whitechapel is the name of the murderer better known as Jack the Ripper.

Part of a Ripper Letter
From Liverpool Received
after the Double Murder of
30th September 1888

"What fools the police are. I even give them
the name of the street where I am living".

The second letter refers to the Ripper letter of 29th September
1888. The first sentences in both letters can make an anagram
of Walter. The name of the street is Cleveland Street. In the
letter of 29th September, the numbers for Cleveland are 5, 5, 5,
5, 4, 3, 3, 3, 3. "BUT THERE IS" is an anagram of STREET.
  Words used,

chanCe shalL therE twelVe nevEr poLiceman

neAr miNories miDnight

The Source of the Writing

Sickert took words, written on the same pages, from Dostoevsky's novel 'Crime and Punishment', and used them to form his chalk message written on the wall, as well as his letters to the police and other letters that he sent.

I have a Heron Books copy with the original translation, and this is the translation that Sickert would have read. I will start with the chalk message written on the wall - THE JUWES ARE THE MEN THAT WILL NOT BE BLAMED FOR NOTHING. In 'Crime and Punishment', the words appear on the following pages:

- page 253, The Jews are the.
- page 260, men that,
- page 266, will not.
- pages 159 and 160, be blame,
- page 434, for nothing
- page 295, that will not be for nothing.

The chalk message decode is:

```
Walter Richard Sickert, based at
Old Montague Street is the name
of the murderer, better known as
Jack the Ripper.
```

The words, "is the of the murderer", are written on page 62; name, page 107; better known, page 329; as, page 328. The following are words from Jack the Ripper's letters to the police: "Ha Ha Ha", "Catch me if you can". On page 183; Ha, ha, ha; if, page 182; catch me you can. The next letter, "Just to give you a little clue" "I told her I was Jack the Ripper and I took my hat off"".

On page247, Just; page 262, to give you; page 3, a little clue; page 325, I told her I was; page 233 and I took my hat off. The next letter, with the heading," Dear Boss", was mailed on July 22nd, 1889. The first two sentences are: "Back again & up to the old tricks. Would you like to catch me? I guess you would well look here". In Dostoevsky' s novel, the words appear as follows: page 149, back again; page 363, and to the old tricks; page 361, up; page 119, Would you to catch me; page 120, like; page 326, I guess you, page 325, would, page 4, well look here.

Another letter began, Reasons for Supposing Jack the ripper a tailor from his letter. Page 212, reasons for, page 220, Supposing, page 3, a tailor, from letter, page 355, his. The letter to Mr Lusk said, Catch me when you can Mishter Lusk. Page 182, catch me when you can. One of Sickert's paintings is called ''Lazarus breaks His Fast". Page 195, Lazarus. Page 202, broken his fast. Another painting was called, Jack the Ripper's Bedroom-this is an anagram of Sickert.

Eight of the first ten words in a Ripper letter are found on page 173- "I shall be in on the of this and will..." The start of the Ripper letter- "I shall be in Whitechapel on the 20th of this month- And will"

If the letter S is added to Jack the Ripper, it is an anagram of Sickert. In some of the letters to the police, an S is placed just in front of Jack the Ripper- e.g. "I told her I was Jack the Ripper and I took my hat off". Another letter ends, "Jack a Poland Jew better known as Jack the Ripper". In another, the last word before Jack the Ripper is "dreams".

Another letter-

```
Dear Boss

You have not caught me yet you
see, with all your cunning, with
all your "Lees" with all your
blue bottles.

Jack the Ripper
```

```
Sickert also used Dumas novel "The Count
of Monte Cristo". In the anonymous letter
of Oct 20th. 1888, "Motive for the Crimes
is hatred and spite against the authorities
of Scotland Yard one of whom is marked as
a victim, the words, one of whom is marked
```

as a victim, are found on page 286 of the Collins Classics Giant Edition. Sickert also did a painting entitled, Amphitryon, with an alternative title, X's Affiliation Order. Amphitryon is found on page 282.

Sickert also used his favourite novel, Dickens, Bleak House, Penguins Classics Edition, Page 109, "I told her I was and I took my hat off.

Did Sickert Base His Character on Raskolnikoff?

The sixth letter in Sickert's full name, Walter Richard Sickert, is R. That is, 666, the devil's number.

The first letter in Raskolnikoff's name, Rodion Romanovitch Raskolnikoff is R also. Raskolnikoff committed a double murder and Sickert committed a double murder.

Raskolnikoff wore a neckerchief and so did Sickert, and a man seen with a Ripper victim shortly before she was murdered wore a neckerchief also. This was Catherine Eddowes.

Did Sickert hate Sir Charles Warren, Commissioner of the Metropolitan Police? Did Sickert believe that he was a genius and extraordinary man who had a right to commit murder? The following is taken from 'Crime and Punishment'.

"Fancy, Rodia, the discussion last evening turned on the question: 'Does crime exist? Yes, or No.' And the nonsense they talked on the subject!"

"What is there extraordinary in the query? It is the social question without the charm of novelty," answered Raskolnikoff abruptly.

"The question was not put like that," remarked Porphyrius.

"Not exactly like that, I own", Razoumikhin immediately admitted, who had moved according to his wont. "Listen, Rodia, and give us your opinion - I insist. Yesterday, when those fellows upset me, and I was expecting you, having told them you were coming - these Socialists then commenced by airing their theory. We all know what it is - in other words, crime is a protest against a badly organised social state of things - that's all. When they have said that, they have said all; they admit no other cause for criminal acts; in their own opinion, man is driven to commit crime in consequence of the irresistible influence of the environment, and nothing else. This is their favourite theme."

"Talking of crime and environment" said Porphyrius Petrovitch, speaking to Raskolnikoff, "I remember a production of yours which greatly interested me. I am speaking about your article 'On Crime'- I don't very well remember the title. I was delighted in reading it two months ago in the Periodical Word."

"My article? In the Periodical Word?" asked Raskolnikoff, astonished. "I wrote, it is true, an article six months ago, when I left the University, in connection with some book, but I sent it to the Hebdomadal Word, and not to the Periodical Word."
"That is the paper it came out in."

"In the meantime, the Hebdomadal Word ceased to appear; that was why my article was not published at the time." Quite so, but, whilst no longer appearing, the Hebdomadal Word became amalgamated with the Periodical Word, and this is how your article was published by the latter paper two months ago. Did you not know that?" Raskolnikoff had not known it.

"Then you may go and draw the money for your copy! What a disposition is yours however! You live so hermit-like that the very things which interest you directly, do not even come under your notice! That is a fact." "Bravo, Rodia! I did not know anything about it either!" exclaimed Razoumikhin. "This very day I shall ask for the number in the reading-room! Is it two months ago since the article was inserted? What was the date? Never mind - 1 shall find out! What a joke! And he has never said anything about it!" "But how do you know the article was mine? I only signed it with an initial."

"I discovered it lately, quite by chance. The chief editor is a friend of mine; it was he who let out the secret of your authorship. The article has greatly interested me."

"I was analysing, if I remember rightly, the psychological condition of a criminal at the moment of his deed" "Yes, and you strove to prove that a criminal, at such a moment, is always, mentally, more or less unhinged. That point of view is a very original one, but it was not this part of your article which most interested me. I was particularly struck by an idea at the end of the article, and which, unfortunately, you have touched upon too cursorily. In a word, if you remember, you maintained that there are men in existence who can, or more accurately, who have an absolute right to commit all kinds of wicked, and criminal acts- men for whom, to a certain extent, laws do not exist." -

At this false interpretation of his views, Raskolnikoff smiled.

"How? What? A right to commit crime? Did he not rather mean to say that a criminal is urged to crime by the irresistible centrifugal influence?" asked Razoumikhin with a species of anxiety.

"No, no, that is not the point in question," replied Porphyrius. "In the article under discussion, men are divided into ordinary and extraordinary men. The former must live in a state of obedience, and have no right to break the law, inasmuch as they are nothing more than ordinary men; the latter have a right to commit every kind of crime and to break every law, from the very fact that they are extraordinary men.

I think that is what you mean, unless I am mistaken?"

"But how? It is impossible that such things can be!" stammered Razoumikhin, confused. Raskolnikoff smiled again. He had seen in a moment that they wished to get from him a statement of facts, and remembering his article, he was ready to enter into explanations. "That is not quite it," he commenced in simple and modest tones. "I must allow, however, that you have almost precisely reproduced my theory; if you like, I will go so far as to say, very precisely"(he emphasised these last words with a certain pleasure). "I did not say, however, as you make me do, that extraordinary men are absolutely bound to be always committing all kinds of criminal acts. I even believe that the censor would not have permitted the publication of an article conceived in that sense. This is really what I maintained: An extraordinary man has a right - not officially, be it understood, but from and by his very individuality - to permit his conscience to overstep certain bounds, only so far as the realisation of one of his ideas may require it. (Such an idea may from time to time be of advantage to humanity.) You pretend that my article is not a clear one; I will do my best to make it so; perhaps I am right in surmising that such is your wish. According to my theory, if Kepler's or Newton's inventions had, in consequence of certain obstacles, not been able to get into vogue without the sacrifice of one, ten, a hundred, or even a larger number of intervening human impediments, Newton would have had the right - nay, would have been obliged - to do away with these few, these hundred men, in order that his discoveries might become known to the whole world. This does not imply, however, that Newton had a right to assassinate at his will or fancy any living thing, or to steal daily in the open market.

"Further on in my article, I remember insisting on the idea that all legislators and rulers of men, commencing with the earliest down to Lycurgus, Solon, Mahomet, Napoleon, etc. etc., have one and all been criminals, for, whilst giving new laws, they have naturally broken through older ones which had been faithfully observed by society and transmitted by its progenitors. These men most certainly never hesitated to shed blood, as soon as they saw the advantage of doing so. It may even be remarked that nearly all these benefactors and teachers of humanity have been terribly bloodthirsty. Consequently, not only all great men, but all those who, by hook or by crook, have raised themselves above the common herd, men who are capable of evolving something new, must, in virtue of their innate power, be undoubtedly criminals, more or less, be it said.

Otherwise they could not free themselves from trammels; and, as for being bound by them, that they cannot be - their very mission forbidding it.

"You must own that, as far as we have gone, there is nothing very new in my article. The same views have been uttered and printed a thousand times. As for my division of men into ordinary and extraordinary ones, I own to its being somewhat arbitrary, but I take no heed of the question of figures, which hampers me but slightly. But I believe that the kernel of my theory is a sound one. It confines itself to maintaining that Nature divides men into two categories: the first, an inferior one, comprising ordinary men, the kind of material whose function it is to reproduce specimens like themselves; the other, a superior one, comprising men who have the gift or power to make a new word, thought or deed felt. Their sub-divisions are naturally innumerable, but these two main categories contain distinctively marked characteristics. To the first belong, in a general way, , conservatives, men for order, who live in a state of obedience and love. To my mind, such men cannot help obeying, because it is their destiny, and such an act has nothing humiliating for them.

"The next class, however, consists exclusively of men who break the law, or strive, according to their capacity or power, to do so. Their crimes are naturally relative ones, and of varied gravity. Most of these insist upon destruction of what exists in the name of what ought to exist. And if, in the execution of their idea, they should be obliged to shed blood, step over corpses, they can conscientiously do both in the interest of their idea, not otherwise - pray mark this. It is in so far that my article gives them a right to commit crime. (You will remember that our starting argument was a judicial question.) There is, however, not much need for anxiety. The mass of men hardly ever concedes them such a right; it either decapitates or hangs them, and by doing so performs most virtuously its conservative mission till the day this very class erects statues in veneration of those thus executed. The first group is always predominant in the present; the second, however, is master of the future. One class keeps up the world by increasing its inhabitants, the other arouses humanity and makes it act. Both have absolutely the same right to existence- yea, even to the day of the New Jerusalem!"

"Then you believe in the New Jerusalem!"

"I do," replied, with considerable stress, Raskolnikoff, who, during the whole of this tirade, had kept his eye obstinately fixed on some spot in the carpet.

"And - do you believe in God? Excuse my inquisitiveness."

"I do," repeated the young man, raising his eyes on Porphyrius. " And in the resurrection of Lazarus?"

"Yes. But why put such questions?" "Do you believe fully?"
"Fully."

"Excuse me having put these questions, but I was interested. Permit me once more - I am going back to the subject we were talking about just now - they are not always executed; on the contrary, there are some who ... " "What? Who are triumphant during their lifetime? Yes, such a thing happens to some of them, and then ... " "It is they, I suppose, who give up the others for capital punishment?"

"Yes, if necessary, and, let me tell you, this is most frequently the case. From a general point of view, your observation is full of accuracy." "Thanks. But tell me: How is it possible to distinguish these extraordinary men from ordinary ones? Have they, at birth, any special marks? It strikes me that here we require a little more precision, and, to some extent, a more apparent definition. Excuse this fidgetiness, after all but natural to a practical and well-meaning man; but could they not, for instance, wear some special dress - an emblem of some kind or other? For, you must agree, if confusion set in; if a member of one class were to conceive that he belonged to the other, and were, according to your happy expression, to try and 'overcome every obstacle,' then ... " "Oh! Such a thing often happens. Your second remark is even a more clever one than the other."

"Thanks!"

"Don't mention it; but remember that such an error is only possible with men of the first category, that is to say, in the case of those whom I have, perhaps clumsily, called 'ordinary' men. Notwithstanding their inborn tendency to obey, many of them , as a result of some freak of nature, fancy themselves men that ought to be in the van, and consider themselves in the light of 'regenerators' think themselves selected to bring about a 'new state of things,' and this illusion is perfectly genuine in their case. At the same time, they do not, as a rule, recognise the real regenerators, they even sometimes despise them as people behind the times - lacking in genius. But in my opinion that is not a very great danger, and there is no occasion for anxiety, for they never accomplish much. They may sometimes be urged on by way of punishment for their presumption, and thus be placed once more in their right place, but that is all; even in such cases, there is no special need to harass the instrument - on the contrary, they themselves are more or less their own castigators, because their characters are sensitive ones, and this punishment they either award each other mutually or by themselves. They may be seen undergoing various open inflictions, which cannot fail to edify; in a word, anxiety on their score would be more than futile." "I must confess that in this particular case you have somewhat set me at rest, but here is something else which worries me; tell me, pray, are there many of these extraordinary men who have the right to destroy others? I am ready to yield their precedence, but if there are very many of them, you must own such a fact to be rather a disagreeable one, eh?"

"Pray do not let that disturb you to any great extent, Raskolnikoff continued in the same tone. "Generally, the number of men born with new ideas, or even capable of giving utterance to anything out of the ordinary course, is infinitesimal. It is a self-evident fact that the repartition of births in the various categories and subdivisions of humanity must be carefully regulated by some natural law. This law, unfortunately, is unknown to us as yet, but I fully believe in its existence and also that it will be discovered sooner or later. I believe that very many of us have only one duty in this world, the bringing finally into existence, after long and mysterious crossbreeding, one man out of a thousand with a trace of independence. In proportion to this increase of independence, we begin to discover one man in ten thousand, or even in a hundred thousand (my figures are approximate ones). A genius is found among several millions of men, and it is highly probable that thousands of millions pass through life before there arises one of those lofty intellects which renew the face of the globe.

Unfortunately, I have had no opportunity of peeping in the retort where this process of evolution takes place. At all events there is, there must be some immutable law at work in this process - chance has nothing whatever to do with it."

"I really think that both of you are joking," exclaimed, at last, Razumikhin; "you are mystifying one another, I fancy! You are not really talking seriously, are you, Rodia?"

Without replying, Raskolnikoff raised on him his pale and apparently suffering face. Whilst looking at its calm and woebegone expression, Razoumikhin thought the caustic, irritating, and rude manner Porphyrius had assumed was very singular.

"Well, my dear friend, if you are really serious, of course you are perfectly right in saying that your statements are not new ones, and that they are very much like what we have read and heard a thousand times; but I am grieved to observe that the only original opinion you adduce, is a moral right to shed blood - this opinion I find you support, even defend, with fanaticism. This is, in fact, the main point of your article. Moral licence or authority to kill is, to my mind, even more terrible than official legal authority to the same effect."

"Quite so. It is, in fact, much more terrible," remarked Porphyrius.

"No, you said more than you really thought; you did not mean that at all!

I purpose reading your article; whilst talking, people are sometimes carried away! You cannot really have such opinions.

But I shall read it." "There is nothing of the kind in my article at all, I have hardly touched upon such a question," said Raskolnikoff.

"Yes, yes," went on Porphyrius, "I now almost understand your way of looking at crime; but, excuse my persistency, if a young man fancies himself a Lycurgus or a Mahomet of the future, of course his first step will be to trample under foot every obstacle in the way of his crusade." "He will say to himself, 'I propose undertaking a long campaign, and, in order to do so, I shall require money. And then, of course, he will get money. Can you guess how?"

All at once, Zametoff sniffed in his corner. Raskolnikoff did not even look at him. "I must admit," he added coolly, "that such cases occasionally occur.

They are snares set by vanity for vain and foolish people; young men especially are caught in them." "You understand that, do you?"

"What?" replied Raskolnikoff with a smile. "Is that my fault? Things of that kind happen every day. Just now," he added, pointing to Razoumikhin, "this man reproached me for countenancing murder. What can that matter? Is society not sufficiently protected by penal servitude, prisons, magistrates, the hulks? Why, therefore, be uneasy? "Find your thief first!"

"And supposing we do find him?" "All the worse for him, of course."

"At all events, you are logical. But what will his conscience tell you?" "What is that to you?"

"It is a question of interest to humanity."

"The man who has a conscience suffers whilst acknowledging his sin. That is his punishment - to say nothing of the galleys."

"Then I suppose," asked Razoumikhin, "men of genius, who have a right to kill, can experience no anguish, even when doing so?"

"Why introduce here the word 'can'? Suffering is neither permitted or forbidden in their case. They may suffer, if they pity their victim. Suffering is part and parcel of extensive intelligence and a feeling heart. A man who is really great, it seems to me, must suffer considerably here below," added Raskolnikoff, affected with sudden melancholy which contrasted with his manner in the course of the preceding conversation. He looked up, regarded the others with dreamy eye, smiled and took his cap. His manner was much too calm, when compared with his bearing on entering the house, and he remembered it. Everyone rose. Once more Porphyrius Petrovitch touched upon the late discussion.

"One moment, if you please, taunt me or not, get angry or not, but -I want to ask one more trifling question. I am ashamed to trespass as I am doing - now that I am on the subject, and in order that I may not forget it, I should like to communicate to you a small idea which has struck me ... "

"All right, out with your small idea!" replied Raskolnikoff, facing the magistrate with a pale and serious countenance.

"I - really -I - hardly know how to express myself. My idea is a singular - psychological one. Whilst composing your article, it is very probable - ha! ha! - that you looked upon yourself in the light of one of those 'extraordinary' men you were talking about. Am I right?"

"Very likely," scornfully responded Raskolnikoff Razoumikhin made a movement.

"If I am right - would you not be induced yourself- either with a view to triumph over material embarrassments, or to assist humanity in its onward course - I say would you not be induced - to step over obstacles? For instance, to kill and to rob?" At the same time, he winked his left eye, and laughed silently, as he had done just before.

"If I were induced to do so, I should certainly not tell you," answered Raskolnikoff, with an accent of haughty disdain.

"Only a kind of literary inquisitiveness induced me to put my question; all I wanted was to get a better grip of the real meaning of your article." "What an obvious trap! What shallow cunning!" thought Raskolnikoff in disgust. "Permit me to observe," he replied curtly, "that I neither consider myself a Mahomet nor a Napoleon, nor anyone like them; consequently I am not in a position to enlighten you as to what I should do if I were in their shoes."

"Come now! Where is the man who at this time, in this country, does not look upon himself as a Napoleon?" retorted the magistrate, with brusque familiarity. The very intonation of his voice savoured of mental reserve.

"Is it not very likely that some coming Napoleon did for Alena Ivanovna last week?" suddenly blustered Zametoff from his corner.

Without saying a word, Raskolnikoff fixed on Porphyrius a firm and penetrating glance. Raskolnikoff was beginning to look sullen. He seemed to have been suspecting something for some time in the past. He looked round him with an irritable air. For a moment there was an ominous silence. Raskolnikoff was getting ready to go. "What, are you off already?" asked Porphyrius, kindly offering the young man his hand with extreme affability. "I am delighted to have made your acquaintance. And as for your application, don't be uneasy about it. Write in the way I suggested. Or, perhaps, you had better do this. Come and see me before long-to-morrow, if you like. I shall be here without fail at eleven o'clock. We can make everything right-we'll have a chat- and as you were one of the last that went THERE, you might be able to give some further particulars?" he added, with his friendly smile. "Do you wish to examine me formally?" Raskolnikoff inquired, in an uncomfortable tone.

"Why should I? Such a thing is out of the question. You have misunderstood me. I ought to tell you that I manage to make the most of every opportunity. I have already had a chat with every single person that has been in the habit of pledging things with the old woman- several have given me very useful information-and as you happen to be the last one- By the by," he exclaimed with sudden pleasure, "how lucky I am thinking about it, I was really going to forget it!" (Saying which he turned to Razoumikhin.) "You were almost stunning my ears, the other day, talking about Nikola. Well, I am certain, quite certain, as to his innocence," he went on, once more addressing himself to Raskolnikoff. "But what was to be done? It has been necessary to disturb Dmitri. Now, what I wanted to ask was: On going upstairs-was it not between seven and eight you entered the house?" "Yes," replied Raskolnikoff and he immediately regretted an answer he ought to have avoided.

Well, in going upstairs, between seven and eight, did you not see on the second floor, in one of the rooms where the door was wide open - you remember, I dare say?-did you not see two painters or, at all events, one of the two? They were whitewashing the room, I believe; you must have seen them! The matter is of the utmost importance to them!" "Painters, you say? I saw none," replied Raskolnikoff slowly, trying to sound his memory: for a moment he violently strained it to discover, as quickly as he could, the trap concealed by the magistrate's question. "No, I did not see a single one; I did not even see any room standing open," he went on, delighted at having discovered the trap, "but on the fourth floor I remember noticing that the man lodging on the same landing as Alena Ivanovna was in the act of moving. I remember that very well, as I met some porters carrying a sofa, and I was obliged to back against the wall; but, as for painters, I don't remember seeing a single one-I don't even remember a room that had its door open. No, I saw nothing,"

"But what are you talking about?" all at once exclaimed Razoumikhin, who, till that moment, had attentively listened; "it was on the very day of the murder that painters were busy in that room, while he came there two days previously! Why are you asking that question?"

"Right! I have confused the dates!" cried Porphyrius, tapping his forehead. "Deuce take it! This job makes me lose my head!" he added by way of excuse, and speaking to Raskolnikoff. "It is very important that we should know if anybody saw them in that room between seven and eight. I thought I might have got that information from you without thinking any more about it. I had positively confused the days!"

"You ought to be more attentive!" grumbled Razoumikhin.

These last words were uttered in the anteroom, as Porphyrius very civilly led his visitors to the door. They were gloomy and morose on leaving the house, and had gone some distance before speaking. Raskolnikoff breathed like a man who had just been subjected to a severe trial.

Crime and Punishment

Bibliography

Cornwell, Patricia Daniels. <u>Portrait of a Killer: Jack the Ripper--Case Closed,</u> Putnam's, 2002, ISBN 0399149325, 9780399149320

Dostoyevsky, Fyodor. <u>Crime and Punishment</u>, Heron, 1966, ISBN 1603033874,9781603033879 Knight, Stephen. <u>Jack the Ripper: The Final Solution</u>, George G. Harrap & Co Ltd, 1976, illus., ISBN O 586 04652 6

Underwood, Peter. <u>Jack the Ripper: One Hundred Years of Mystery,</u> Javelin, 1989, ISBN 0713720611, 9780713720617

Begg, Paul. <u>Jack the Ripper: The Definitive History,</u> Pearson Education, 2003, ISBN 1405807121, 9781405807128

Fuller, Jean Overton. <u>Sickert and the Ripper Crimes: An Investigation Into the Relationship Between the Whitechapel Murders of 1888 and the English Tonal Painter Walter Richard Sickert,</u> Mandrake, 1990, ISBN 1869928156, 9781869928155

Wilde, Oscar. The Picture of Dorian, Gray,Plain Label Books, 1908, ISBN 1603037829,9781603037822

McKenna, Neil. The Secret Life of Oscar Wilde, Arrow, 2004, ISBN 0099415453,9780099415459 Ellmann, Richard. Oscar Wilde: A Biography, Penguin Group (Canada), 1987, ISBN 0670814202, 9780670814206

The title of this book has 12 words and 46 letters, the same number of words and letters as the chalk message written on the wall in Coulston Street.